F.E.A.R.L.E.S.S.

Creating and Finding the
Career You Love

SAMANTHA C. DE LA O

DEDICATION

This book is dedicated to all of those who are inspired by my fearless journey. Without your love and support, this book wouldn't have been completed.

Contents

Chapter 1

Who Is Your Author?

"Today's children are tomorrow's leaders."

(Nelson Mandela)

My goal is to help people who are not living life fearlessly. If you are reading this, you may be one of those individuals. I am going to help you become fearless. I will show you how to create the life you have always dreamed about, with a career you only thought possible in movies. Why? Well, there is this crazy thing we call life, and every day we try to grasp a handle on it. How many fearless moves have you made to get a grasp on your own life? Those fearless moves are a part of your career journey.

Hence, finding your career is key to your happiness. Trust me, I've been on the hunt with no guidance or playbook, and you definitely can't Google this shit. I want to help you find your purpose or career, so you can get a jump-start on loving what you do.

In my book, you will learn about self-discovery, which marks the first step in your journey. After taking your first step, you will learn how to surrender and accept the process that unlocks and pushes past fear. Being in tune with your true self will allow your life experiences to unfold and your career to find you. To achieve this, you need to begin applying the tools found in F.E.A.R.L.E.S.S.

F.E.A.R.L.E.S.S. stands for Family & Friends (your network), Energy, Awareness, Risks, Lessons, Effort, Story, and Success. These eight core concepts will serve as your guide.

Now, before diving into the eight core concepts, here is a little bit about me:

I was notoriously bad at writing essays, and constantly got poor grades in English class. Yet, here I am, writing this book. It's hilarious to me.

Even though I still have so much to learn and explore in life, I want to share my knowledge and tell my story and how far I have come through fearlessness. After reading my book, I want you to realize that whatever happens (or has happened) in your life, it does not mean you are alone; someone understands. Someone will empathize with and support you.

I am a 26-year-old woman of Mexican, Italian, and Polish descent, born and raised in Chicago. The real Chicago, not Naperville, Streamwood, Elmhurst, Schaumburg, River Grove, Elmwood Park, not the nice little suburbs near by), along with two beautiful sisters.

My oldest sister, Tabitha, reminds me every day to be patient and respect the process of writing. My little sister Mariah encourages me to be a great role model and first time author. I am the middle child. Think of all your preconceived notions about the middle child: that's me. We do what we want, are great negotiators, and good listeners.

Up to this point, writing my first chapter feels like I'm crafting my dating profile. I am single, but honestly I'm far more focused on my career and self-love at the moment.

As a kid, I was the butterball, but nevertheless, a talented one. From elementary to high school, I stuck with sports. Sports taught me how to work in a team, be accountable, be self-disciplined, and encouraged me to have consistently good grades. Overall, they taught me lessons that I carry with me as a young adult and use in regularly.

Sports and dance were equally valuable tools in my life. My creative side was brought out through learning and performing choreography, and connecting with music. My commitment and consistency was enhanced from team building platforms on and off the court. Whether it was sports or dance, being a performer in your work on the field or on stage, you are representing yourself and your character.

I have never been afraid of hard work, and I believe that participating in all these activities when I was young sculpted my character. As I get older, I feel my character has never changed, but has instead evolved my values and perspectives. I was not born into a Kardashian lifestyle. I have earned everything I own. I put the work in and have made a name for myself. Regardless of how much money you are making and accomplishments you have achieved, putting the work in does not stop. By continuing to work hard, doors of opportunities will start opening.

Before college, I realized I did not want to pursue sports as a career. I saw it as more of a hobby. Realizing this before college began was crucial, because I had the opportunity to play softball on a scholarship instead of diving into a career. As a college freshman, I wanted to become a secondary high school teacher, specifically in mathematics. Though that didn't pan out, I am still great at math. I fell into it basically by accident. When freshmen orientation ended, I saw other students going to another meet-and-greet, for the teaching program. So, I followed a few students to the room and met the professor in charge of the department.

Once the meet-and-greet was over, I spoke to the professor and admitted that I was not really part of the program, but was very interested. The professor was so shocked and amused by my enthusiasm that he took a chance on me. It didn't seem so odd at the time, but in hindsight I realize that this skill came naturally to me. Making the effort to "put yourself out there" and take a risk can create surprising results. Training yourself to do this can be scary at first, but remind yourself that by not working on yourself, you are closing a door of opportunity.

Despite my initial enthusiasm, I decided to change my major after completing two years. My new major became Communications, Media, and Theater, with a double minor in Philosophy and Human Resources development. Changing majors was not as hard for me as I thought it would be. If anything, I was relieved that I knew as a sophomore that I didn't want to become a teacher anymore, instead of after college graduation.

After observing classes, I knew I didn't want to become a teacher anymore. The hands-on experience will show you if you really have the passion for something or not. In my case, I enjoyed it, but I had an internal calling to do more. I had no idea at the time what that was, but I knew it would still be in the arts and communication field.

After changing majors, I decided to make it a priority to do as many internships as I could. It became clear that I needed the hands-on experience to get a clear understanding of what I wanted to do.

My first internship was for Wilson Dow Group/Under The Radar, a pharmaceutical marketing company run by the father of the family I previously nannied for. I asked him if I would be able to visit him at work to learn more about what he did, and he was happy to discuss his journey towards his success. The day ended with an internship offer. This was the second time it became clear that putting myself out there, asking people questions, and letting people know what I was up to, would result in people opening up to offer help, support, and connection. People love helping those who help themselves. Some love talking about themselves, and you have to listen. On the other hand, others don't want to be bossy, and wait for you to ask.

I was grateful for the opportunity, but after completing the internship I discovered that I didn't want anything to do with pharmaceuticals and/or marketing. Instead I really enjoyed being out in the field with the producer/coordinator on location. The next journey I wanted to explore was watching a project develop, from initial pitch to completion.

Once I got a better idea of what interested me, I had a more efficient process when applying to different internships and not applying to just anything. This process helped me narrow down what I wanted to explore. That narrower scope lead me to my next internship at Travel Film Productions.

The two words that caught my attention in the internship description were "travel" and "productions." These were two things that I had started to grow a passion for. I believe it was rooted in the time I spent traveling with my Gift Souls Dance Company, and learning more about production and media from my college courses and internships.

When I found the internship posting online and read the qualifications, I realized I was 100% under-qualified. I didn't care. I still applied and was honest during my interview. My character and work ethic showed through, and the supervisors were as excited to give me a opportunity. This alone was rare, but yet very special for me. With time working in my favor, one internship led to another. I was getting first-hand experience and education on what worked perfect for me.

Before I graduated college, I had four internships under my belt. The insatiable hunger paid off to get as much experience as possible. Learning what did and didn't interest me allowed me to significantly narrow down what I wanted moving forward. My senior year of college, I was sure I wanted to be on the production end of the entertainment industry. Yes, I am now aware when you only mention production that is vague to say. However, I went based off what I knew at the time. Regardless, I packed up my brand new car and left my family, friends, and lover behind to move to Los Angeles by myself.

Los Angeles is the most obvious choice for anyone who wishes to work in show business, so I made the conscious choice on my last spring break to visit the city. When my friends wanted to go to Miami and Cancun, I opted to put my curiosity first and traveled alone to L.A.

My solo spring break consisted of cold-calling as many production companies as possible, sending out countless resumes, going on interviews for summer positions, doing info sessions with managers, and getting the opportunity from a friend to visit a real TV production set. My friend brought me to the MBS Media Campus and took me to the set of "Jane the Virgin." I was able to explore a set for the first time, observe the on-set workflow, and also met the lead, Gina Rodriguez (who is also from Chicago), which made that experience extra special. I decided on my flight back home that I was 100% committed to taking the leap and moving to L.A. after graduation. What led me to this final decision was based off what I knew at the time. Los Angeles was where I would hear and see on televison all movies, T.V. shows, award shows, and movies were shot at. Hence, why I decided L.A. was going to be my fearless move.

Two weeks before graduation, I landed a summer internship to work at Principato Young Entertainment in Beverly Hills. This was one of the companies that I cold-called and visited during my spring break trip. The timing of this couldn't have been more perfect because, a few days prior, I was upset I did not get the position I wanted in a company based out of Santa Monica. I believe everything happens for a reason, and

I've learned that there is a difference between working very hard to achieve something, and forcing something to happen. I ended up exactly where I was meant to be.

Even though I was enjoying the win of getting my first Hollywood internship, a curveball came in hot. The person who was going to rent me a room in Beverly Hills let me know that the room was no longer available. With such short notice, I started to question whether or not to move to Los Angeles. I had reached out to a family friend to ask for support, as I began doubting the decisions I was making. My friend's older sister, Celina, lived about 90 miles from Beverly Hills in a town called Menifee, and was ready to welcome me with open arms. At that point, I released a sigh of relief, and this put me back on the right mental track to make this move to L.A. happen.

I worked at LensCrafters as an Eyecare Advisor as a side job while in college. Who would have thought that staying with the company as long as I did, would create the opportunity to guarantee a job in another state. My plan was only moving forward and I was reminded by an unknown author that dealing with my fears come with reinventing myself.

Starting my new journey in California was exciting, yet very challenging. Realizing neither my family nor my lover were physically there for me anymore was challenging. Driving two hours each way to an internship started to take a toll on my mind and body. I knew this journey was going to be a huge change for me, but it really didn't hit me until two months in. Regardless of the long hours, lengthy commute, and mental battles, what saved me is the fight I had in me to make it happen for myself.

With the internship coming to an end, I learned being an office manager's assistant was not my calling. I was blessed with such a great opportunity and experience from the people I got to work with, but I wanted to dive into other aspects of the entertainment industry. I started to apply for new opportunities and followed up with the companies I met with during my spring break visit.

Going to interview after interview and not getting a job offer was one thing, but the bigger stress was driving back home later and later, going 90 miles each way to and from Menifee. I was beginning to feel as if I was driving under the influence, and it crossed my mind to start sleeping in my car to stop the madness of my commute.

Day 1 of sleeping in my car, I finished my internship and purposefully stayed late to pass time. I attended a comedy event, then drove to the gym to work out and shower. While working out, I figured why not keep my car parked near the gym so when I wake up I can work out again, shower, and then head to my internship. I gave it a shot and did exactly this. I made sure my car was parked in a safe spot, cleared my trunk to put my blanket and pillow in, and then put one back seat down so I could breathe.

After getting situated, I attempted to close my eyes but my thoughts started to travel to anything and everything:

"This is insane!"

"What are you doing?"

"Can I really do this?"

"Are you happy?"

"I want babe. Call babe!"

"Call your sister!"

"The struggle is real!"

"This will all be worth it, and for sure a story to tell."

Through the tears, and after a phone call to my sister, not only did I finally fall asleep, but I also perceived that this would be my first and last time to ever sleep in my car.

After three months of living in California, and my first internship complete, I was onto my next journey with another production company, Eyeboogie. I found an apartment with roommates on Craigslist, in the heart of Hollywood - literally! The apartment was on Hollywood Blvd. and N. Highland Ave, which is central in the area. The move and new job was a constant reminder of why I moved to Los Angeles. It was the best feeling in the world.

Living in L.A. was great. I was now able to really explore the city, meet new people, network, and attend events. By doing so, I learned that there is a significant gap between telling people you are moving to a major city, and your actions when you get there. If you are not getting involved in your new city and/or not taking advantage of the access you have while living there, you're not really living there yet. Your experience when you move to a large new city completely changes when people see that you are staying busy and being productive with your time. You are truly putting yourself out there to find and commit to figuring out what you want to do with your life.

When you are in the mental state of genuinely trying to figure your life out, you truly catch yourself making strides in the right direction. At times, sometimes without even trying, the daily routine you keep will introduce you to new people and experiences. From being at work, at the gym, clubs, bars, or even walking down the street, you start constantly networking.

Networking really fueled me and created many opportunities when I was in Los Angeles. For example, I attended a preconcert for the MTV Music Video Awards, simply by standing in line and looking out for the people with credentials around their neck. I was able to do a quick pitch to them and make a connection.

"Hi, my name is Sammy. I just moved here from Chicago. Here is my business card, and if you ever need additional help for an event, I'd be happy to be on board and help out."

By putting myself out there, I ended up meeting the coordinator who hires a majority of the awards shows in town. Later that evening when I got home, I emailed him my resume right away. My rule of thumb is to always email the person you meet that same day because they have a fresh memory of you, and their conversation with you.

After about six months in L.A., with the new year approaching, I was busy and blessed to still be working with Eyeboogie as Office Coordinator, freelancing as talent escort, and still holding my position as an Eye Care Advisor at Lens-Crafters. The only change after the new year was moving into a new apartment in the Koreatown area. There were no hard feelings between the roommates and I, but I found myself evolving yet again and saw the move as starting a new chapter in my L.A. journey.

With all the great new opportunities happening in L.A. from a new job, apartment, and new network, I decided to spend the holidays in Chicago with family. It was nice to reboot before going back to Los Angeles. It jolted my confidence. I told myself that, even though I didn't get into the Assistant Directors' Training Program I applied for, I wouldn't start my new year beating myself up about it. Instead, I would embrace what I was currently blessed to be working on at Eyeboogie, and would be patient for what my next opportunity would be. Sure enough, another opportunity soon presented itself. Business Rockstars, the company I had tried to get an internship with upon my arrival in L.A., reached out to me to offer a position as Segment Producer and Talent Booker. This company produces incredible interviews with the world's biggest and most accomplished CEO's, billionaires, entrepreneurs, influencers, celebrities, small business owners, innovators, and industry disruptors that airs on several media platforms. The connections I would make through this company under the Co-Founder, Ken Rutkowski, would be invaluable. I knew this was my next step forward in my Los Angeles journey.

My Eyeboogie co-workers were amazing people, and I still stay in contact with many of them today. As I left any job or internship, I always made sure that I wasn't burning bridges, and that I stayed consistently in touch with them. Maintaining communication with people and genuinely caring for my relationships has led to more open doors of opportunities and growth.

Working with Business Rockstars introduced me to the entrepreneurial world. Entrepreneurship started to become a new passion that I found myself really enjoying. By working in the entertainment industry and meeting entrepreneurs at the same time, I was really living in the moment and getting closer to finding my career niche.

When I arrived at my one-year anniversary of living in Los Angeles, a big turning point happened outside of my work world. I found another apartment and gave my security deposit with first and last month's rent, and after giving my current landlord notice of my departure, I learned I was being scammed. I went from talking to the owner of the new apartment every day, to getting no response from him for days. This was all happening less than two weeks from my move-in date. My stress level was through the roof.

Managing a live TV show and figuring out where to live at the same time was a level of anxiety I hope no one ever has to experience. Without my family and friends' support, I wouldn't have pulled through it. Thanks to my networking skills, I met someone at the right time and place while working at LensCrafters: a lawyer.

This is a customer I will never forget. After expressing to her my current apartment scam situation, she offered to help me. She ended up writing an official certified letter to the sleazy landlord and he responded so quickly I couldn't believe it. I had *all* of my money transferred back to my account the next morning. I was so blessed to have met this customer and cried countless tears of joy. Honestly, what are the odds of meeting a lawyer at work and her willingness to help me for no charge at the exact time that I needed it?

The beauty of timing and how things end up falling together in life are one of the many lessons I have learned through my L.A. journey. Due to the mental hardship, I did start getting uninspired because of the mental energy that got drained from getting scammed. However, by remembering I am human and it is okay not to be okay, my personal puzzle pieces (finances, work, and housing) started to come back together again.

Even though things started to align again, I started to experience a new type of emotion. I noticed during my day-to-day routine that I started to feel unfulfilled. The best way to explain this feeling is as though something is missing, with no particular reason to point to. It wasn't a forgetful feeling, like you misplaced your phone or missed your ex. It was a feeling beyond this.

I started to question why I would be feeling this, especially as I became financially stable, had an apartment, and my family and friends were doing great. The result of feeling this (realizing this feeling was an existential crisis that was happening subconsciously in my mind) for two months, led to my decision to leave Los Angeles, and find what was missing elsewhere.

I decided to move back to Chicago. I gave myself a deadline to only stay in Chicago until the end of the summer. It was important for me to make a deadline for myself. I can honestly say that if I hadn't, I would still be living in Chicago, secure in my comfort zone.

Even though I was moving back home, it still was a change for me. After college, I never tried to make it in the entertainment industry in my own city. I went straight to Hollywood. I was looking forward to the upcoming summer, and being close to family and friends, while exploring my own potential in Chicago.

I wasn't distracted as much as I thought I would be while so close to family. If anything, I quickly confirmed that Chicago is not nearly as busy in the entertainment industry compared to Los Angeles. I put my all into getting work on TV, film, and commercials, but it just wasn't happening for me. When summer was coming to an end, I ended up booking a cheap $90 round-trip flight to New York. This trip was to visit a friend in the Big Apple, but also wound up being a glimpse into my next big adventure.

Visiting New York for the first time was amazing. The feeling of being there was the same feeling I experienced when I first visited Los Angeles. The energy, the culture, the busyness, and overall vibe. I fell in love with New York.

This trip turned into something I never would have expected. After going back to Chicago, I officially decided my next city move was to New York. It only took me one month to get there after my trip.

When I got to the airport in Chicago, right before check in, I realized I couldn't find my driver's license. In that moment, I questioned myself. I tend to find signs and overthink everything. Was this a sign for me not to go to New York?

Sign or not, without my driver's license, I wouldn't be able to travel. After panicking and searching frantically, I did end up finding it. I found it on the floor of the terminal where I was dropped off. When the panic subsided, I also realized I had my passport on me, so I actually would have been fine either way. The power of a doubting mind can take over me. Its starts with overthinking everything. Then, it leads to panic. Once I feel panic I mentally transition into a dark thought process.

From a self-realization perspective, it is important how long I allowed myself to feel a certain way. I consciously allowed my mind to take over. Self-realization is a beautiful thing.

My first New York home was in Chestnut Ridge (Upstate), with the Chase family. Serena, a Chicago dance-family friend of mine, introduced me to her aunt and cousin. They opened up their home for me to stay until I landed a production job in New York City.

Chestnut Ridge is roughly one hour away from Manhattan. This time around, I did not have my car. I decided to leave it in Chicago, because I was told having a car New York is incredibly expensive and there is a great transportation system to utilize. It didn't take me long to become a pro at taking the train or bus into the city.

Similar to when I first traveled to Los Angeles, I had LensCrafters transfer me to a New York store. It ended up being a great location and team. Aside from my eyecare role and knowing I wanted to find jobs in production, I was starting from scratch. I began my cold-calling process, just the same as I did in Los Angeles. The outcome of the cold-calling went great! My resumes were being sent to several production companies, and I had meet-and-greets or interviews set up for the upcoming week.

Moving to another major city for the second time, I was not home sick this time around. My cold-calling process was easier for me. The best thing about this was not only did I notice my improved confidence, but my family and friends did as well.

Two weeks into my New York move, I still hadn't landed a production gig yet. However, what I loved about the process of searching was exploring the city. The culture, vibe, and architecture had me falling in love with Manhattan every day.

While exploring, I started to notice a lot of production permits, production trucks, and crew with walkie-talkies. At the time, I genuinely had no idea what to say or whom to approach. However, I decided in that moment to take a risk and just do it. I took a deep breath, went up to the crew and knocked on production truck doors to introduce myself. My pitch this time was a little stronger.

"My name is Sammy and I just moved to New York. I did P.A. work in both Chicago and L.A., so if you ever need an additional P.A., here is my information."

Reaching out to crew on set and approaching production trucks like this was effective in getting me work within a week. I was booked on my first union TV show, Quantico, as an additional Production Assistant. The crew member that led me to this particular opportunity was Jon Shaw.

I will never forget him because he took a chance on me when I went knocking blindly on doors at Union Square. He saw something in me and passed my information along to the Key P.A. on set to make it possible. I was beyond blessed and filled with a huge amount of happiness by getting booked on a union TV Show within one month of living in New York.

I had no idea what to expect, because I was never a Set Production Assistant before. All I knew from Jon was that I was going to be, "thrown in the deep end to see how well I swim!"

I can proudly say that I survived my first day working on set. But most importantly, my first day helped me decide the career path to work towards. It became clear that my next step was to become a 1st Assistant Director.

October of 2019 will be my three-year mark living in New York. I recently just moved into Manhattan, but was previously living in Brooklyn for my first year in a half. Aside from my living situation, I am also approaching 450 days working as a Set Production Assistant. Once I hit 600 days working as a Set

Production Assistant. I will submit my production P.A. book to the New York office of the Directors Guild of America (DGA). It wasn't so long ago that I was so disappointed not to be accepted into a DGA training program in L.A., but now I am on track to submit my production P.A. book to the New York office. It's funny how timing and patience goes so far.

Working in the entertainment profession is, by far, one of the best decisions I have made. Yes, the production hours are pretty insane and will take a toll on your body. But, if you love what you do, it is easy to look more at the pros than the cons.

Every day, I continue to strive forward and appreciate the people I have been blessed to have both worked with, and learned from. I made mistakes, learned something new every day, and created a family-like support system for myself.

After college, I was on a mission to find out what exactly I wanted my presence in the entertainment industry to be. Three cities, countless job titles and internships, and many growing pains later, I finally got my answer from my fearless journey.

CHAPTER 2

FAMILY & FRIENDS /
YOUR NETWORK

*"You can choose your friends but you sho'
can't choose your family."*

(Harper Lee)

Are you an only child? Do you have siblings? Do you have a big or small family? Are you close with your family? Do you have cousins that live in the same city as you? Are you close in age with your cousins? Who out of your friends have you known the longest? Do you currently have any mentors in your life outside of your family? If so, how did you meet them? Are you meeting new people? What is your process of meeting new people?

The reason I am asking all these questions is for you, to question yourself. Whom are you surrounding yourself with?

Now that you know my story, you can see how the "right" people became an important key factor to stay on track towards the life and career I wanted. I was able to make bold moves to new places but would never have gotten the opportunities I did – in any city – without the help of others. I've learned that who you surround yourself with is very important. Anyone that is bringing you down, or preventing you from pursuing your dream, is not worth your time or energy. Cut them out of your life, now.

You are your own instrument. Anyone who keeps you from playing that instrument needs to be escorted out the back door. Your own thoughts can also cause you harm and prevent you from performing to sold out concerts. In the process of self-discovery, there may be moments where you forget how far you have come. Therefore, take charge of who you want to attract to your concerts, and prepare yourself mentally, physically, and emotionally for your set performances.

In the next chapter, you will learn to create solutions to prevent these negative thought patterns and to take back control of your thought process. Let the music play on. For now, we'll focus on outside influences (the people lining up at the door to hear you play).

Surrounding yourself with people that hold you accountable, make you laugh, and encourage you to be the best version of yourself, are vital to your success. Keep every single one of those people you come across close, and shower them with gratitude.

With social media evolving, we often glorify social influencers with likes and followers. Along with, we tend to forget to thank the influencers who physically surround us. Do what you can to build these relationships for a lifetime.

Small, simple habits may be all that's needed to build these relationships. Remember their birthdays and reach out during holidays. This goes a long way, and can make you stand out from the rest.

Despite the experiences that made you cautious throughout life, always listen to your gut feeling. Trusting your gut is a crucial tool that will forever help you make those tough judgement calls, in both your personal and career decisions.

Draw that line with people if you need to. Know who is family and who is not. By doing this, your trust with your connections will build. Build their trust in you to the extent that, as actor Allen Maldonado once said, "they will never put themselves over you." At the end of the day, you and the other person should always have each other's best interest at heart, particularly when it comes to giving advice and support.

For instance, Allen, who I have been blessed to have worked with on both season one and two on the TV show, "The Last O.G.", mentioned he has been in tune with himself and aware of who he is for a very long time. Therefore, his circle of those he trusts has been the same for a long period of time as well. Regardless how big or small his circle is, he prepared himself for the amount of success he is receiving. For example, Allen distanced himself early on from people in his neighborhood that were bad influences and dead weight, so he could succeed. His way of deciding who he keeps in his inner circle was built in a very strong and long-term process.

IN THE WORKPLACE:

In your work or industry, are you networking with your co-workers? If you are not, today is the day you start. Regardless of what industry you work in, if you are in your dream job or not, train yourself to start building those relationships. Your colleagues are invaluable.

For example, even though my primary field of work is production where I am surrounded by directors, producers, and other cast and crew members, I always try to introduce myself to everyone. Whether I have a staffed position, or I am only on set for a single day, I ensure there are at least four key players who know my name before we wrap for the day. These are the influencers I can not only learn from, but they are also key stake-holders who can help me get my next gig, and open doors to new opportunities.

Another example is from my retail experience. Aside from helping my customers, getting to know them is also something I've trained myself to do very well. You never know what people do for a living, or who people know without asking them. Ask and you shall receive.

From here on out, I challenge you to learn who your co-workers, clients, and customers are, and build those relationships. You will be surprised what doors they can open up. Yes, networking can be uncomfortable and exhuasting, whether you never network, or if you network in every area of your life. But I can guarantee you, it will be worth it.

How do I know for sure?

I recently started forgetting to network as much as I did when I first came to New York. I started to become comfortable where I was in life and, as a result, I started lacking the drive to put myself out there more. It didn't necessarily hurt me, but I did lose out on some possible opportunities.

Nevertheless, I didn't beat myself up for it. Instead, I learned to make sure I am meeting at least one new person each week. Whether it is asking a person I already knew for a connection, or simply talking to someone new on set. It is up to you to decide how you play your network game.

Even though we all keep busy and have crazy schedules, and time passes by quickly, I cannot be anything but grateful to the people who I have connected with throughout the years. I've opened up doors I never would have experienced, if it was not for networking. I'm so thankful to have had the support, kind words, and memorable conversations with countless crew members, celebrities, and talented entertainment influencers.

Everyone I've encountered were all from different production experiences. All have been a part of my growing experiences in my career and fearless journey. For example, my co-workers have all allowed me to pick their brains and ask questions. By doing this, not only am I making sure I am doing what I got hired to do, but I am also making my job a learning experience as well.

Learning and knowing more about the industry you love from different departments and perspectives, will only enhance your skills. Therefore, start looking at your job as a classroom. If you hate the class, leave your job. Do not waste your valuable time and learning energy. But if you absolutely love your class, start looking at your bosses and co-workers as teachers and classmates.

The hours of production are typically a 12 hour work day. Honestly, you spend more time with the cast and crew than your own family. Therefore, they become your family. Within this family you have dedicated valuable time. Value it. Cherish it.

I valued and cherished it so much because I never knew who the next cast and or crew member I would be working with, or if I would work with them again. If I got comfortable enough, my question to an actor was, "what would be your advice to a 26-year old, knowing what you know now?"

I did not ask every actor this, but those I did gave very poignant responses. They said things like:

- "Be nice."
- "Be aware who your enemies are."
- "Be happy and be aware of what makes you happy."
- "When you tell your mind and world what you want, it will happen for you."
- "Don't lose your smile."
- "Stay humble."
- "Really live in your moments."
- "Don't let you get in the way of yourself."

Aside from these nuggets of wisdom, being on set with them taught me to always think positive. There were actors and crew members who told me I was going to be their boss one day. People that have been in the industry for years, were telling me that I had massive potential! To hear this statement from them only enhances my work ethic to new heights, and encourages me to be consistent with my craft.

What type of compliments do you get from people? Are you getting compliments from people? What kind of compliments are they? Are you getting more compliments from family than your co-workers? Strive to be someone who people can't help but acknowledge – but knowing it is important to acknowledge. However, it is also important to acknowledge yourself, and not put your self-worth in the validation of others.

Through my personal journey, I have noticed a consistent pattern when it comes to family influencing my career decisions. Sometimes your family doesn't know what's actually best for you. For example, if I told my family I was planning on moving back to Chicago, 99% of them would support me in this decision, because I haven't lived in Chicago for almost three years.

However, if I mentioned to one of my mentors that I planned on leaving New York to go return to Chicago, they would tell me not to do it. Non-family members who have become close through our work connections and experiences, will have a clearer picture of what is in our best interest. They will be the ones to tell you that going back home will be going back to your comfort zone.

I believe your comfort zone is one of your sacred places. Knowing where your comfort zones lie is important. This knowledge is a great gift, because you are consciously aware when you are stepping toward potential growing pains. With this said, since family is often a part of your comfort zone, they are often blinded by different intentions.

It is always great to have your family, friends, and mentors close. However, it is also important to know who is the most objective and best situation-informed advisor. Creating your relationships is one thing. Creating that boundary for yourself to protect your fearless journey is just as important.

You may be wondering why all this work to maintain relationships with friends, family, and mentors is in your best interest, when it can be so time consuming and sometimes confusing. Why do it? Why should I allow anyone in my fearless journey? Especially if you have to be taking care of yourself, and giving yourself time.

However, I have learned I can't do it all by myself. Yes, it is in my hands what direction I take, and how I manage my time and my work ethic. But, when it comes to accomplishing something and sharing it with family, friends, and mentors, now this is the best feeling in the world.

I have been alone, moving city to city, training myself, and putting everything I have into my work. I am alone in the big city more than enough time throughout the year. Being able to share accomplishments with people I love, and who support me, is just as important.

Don't be afraid to allow people in your life. Simply be wary of their role, and how close to keep them. Live in your moments and appreciate the people in them when you can. Turn off your remote control within in yourself, and let life be.

Determining how close to keep people in your life, and maintaining these relationships can be a challenge. Just like any other obstacle, battle, or argument in life, you will learn from it and apply what you have learned towards your next work and/ or personal relationship. To reiterate, the challenge is worth it, and it determines your successes for your future. Save your energy for the bigger challenges.

As a woman of Mexican, Italian, and Polish descent, I have a big family. When it comes to mentors and friends, I also have a large group of mentors and friends. I have maybe six people in my inner circle, those who I consistently, and regularly, keep close. No matter the number, I value these six people in my life very much. I value them to the extent where I can trust these individuals for the harder decisions I have to make in my life when reaching my goals.

I want you to take a step back and ask yourself—who can't you imagine yourself living without? When you receive good news, who are your first three calls to? Who gives you the exact words you need to hear, when you need to hear them? Who is your #1 fan? And who has been there for you through thick and thin?

When you need someone, who will answer your calls no matter what time it is? Who gives you advice to help you make tough decisions? Who reminds you how you want to spend the rest of your life? Write their names down as they come to you. I will confidently guess you have one to eight people on this list. That's your inner circle.

When it comes to your inner circle, there is no reason to enlarge it. Mine is six, but this doesn't mean everyone has exactly six people. Maybe you only wrote 3 people's names down. This doesn't mean you need to add three more people to your inner circle. I believe the amount of people in your inner circle can vary.

Your network and inner circle are a product of four layers of people in your life, and the way you relate to them.

First layer: yourself

Second layer: your most trusted 1-8 people you keep closest

Third layer: your mentors, additional friends, and networks

Fourth layer: people who come into your life at the right time

No matter how many names there are, keep this circle special. Your **first layer** is you and only YOU. Make sure the people who are in the inner circle feel special - this inner circle is your **second layer.** Allow the people that are in your second layer to remind you of your vision to always keep you moving forward.

Third layer: This layer is made up of those who you have known for quite a while, and continue to support you both in personal events, such as team sports, award ceremonies, reunions, and/or your social media. You may often see these people at social events. Depending how many mentors you have in your life, and your frequency of contact, your mentors can be in either your second or third layer.

Fourth Layer: This layer is full of people you meet at networking events, and/or people you have met out of the blue. This also includes people that have left your life, and then reconnected with again. It is your decision to keep them in this layer and/or bring them closer.

For instance, reconnecting with someone again when it came to writing this book is an example of connecting to people at the right time. Alicia Dunams, someone I haven't talked to since I left Los Angeles but was a mentor for me - was going to be in town for a book workshop. I had been toying with the idea of writing a book. At the time I saw this as a sign from the universe to reconnect with her. With the help of my gut feeling this was the right decision for me. This sign allowed myself to be open minded that this was my time. My schedule aligned perfectly to take this opportunity to begin my book journey. I believe signs like this don't just happen.

Just as life goes on and people continue coming in and out of our lives, it is normal when they move within your number layer system. They can move layer to layer or even out of your circle completely. Regardless let you, and only you, manage where people fall on the spectrum. Have a firm grasp on it, because as you grow, you will learn that it is okay to let people go. People simply grow apart.

A while back, I was blessed and honored to have gotten to interview actor Amaury Nolasco. I clearly remember him talking about his thoughts on family and friends, and the part they played in his fearless journey. He said he never wanted to put family out, because he loves them dearly, but his friends are his support system, when it comes to his career. Like any family, his can be over protective, and care too much, in a way that could lead him to not being his best. He found they were not the best support system because their vision of his life didn't match the one he had for himself.

Amaury's true passion, and love, is acting. As it happens to be a career that is notoriously financially unreliable when you first start out, his friends are his go-to support system when it comes to bad news. He knows they will be there for him when he needs to vent, because his friends will always be objective to

CHAPTER 3

ENERGY

"Everything is energy and that's all there is to it.
Match the frequency of the reality you want and you
cannot help but get that reality..."

(Darryl Anka)

Energy is a moving concept. Moving concepts come in two forms: positive energy and negative energy. I was intrigued during my interview with actor Allen Maldonado, when he said "energy only moves". It reminded me that life always moves and goes on.

Allen also mentioned that in order to give off positive energy for people to absorb, you personally need to be in a positive state of mind. For Allen, positive energy has allowed him to pursue forward in his career leaps.

When you walk into a room, can you sense the energy of it? I've learned that the more I am in tune with myself, the better I am able to sense the energy in an environment, and/or the people around me. Being in tune with yourself and what you need opens your ability to connect with your energy, which can then allow your journey to unfold more smoothly. What you are putting out there reflects who you keep company with, who you attract, the type of conversations you are having, and who you stay away from.

Whether you are currently in tune with yourself or not, I want you to be aware of what type of energy you are personally putting out to the world. A great starting point can simply be asking people in your first and/or second layer what type of energy you bring into a room. Is your energy positive or negative. Make sure the people you ask are the people who will be very honest with you. You cannot learn if you need to make changes if someone is being kind instead of honest.

The purpose of observing the energy in a room is so you are aware of it. When you are of it, you can learn and let the creative space in your mind to listen and connect with people you are meeting. The creative space in your mind will turn everything you are listening to, and observing into knowledge. This knowledge will become valuable to you in your future conversations.

When you meet groups of people for the first time, are you the one leading the conversations? Or are you the quiet one, just observing and listening?

I was often given the advice to listen and not speak. Why? So I can learn not only someone's body language, but also absorb and fully immerse myself with everything that people are talking about.

Managing your energy is one thing, but balancing your energy when life throws a curveball is another. Have you ever allowed an argument to ruin your day? Has a person's bad attitude influenced a rough day for you? Or have you ever woken up late and been upset with yourself, setting the tone of your day with frustration? If the answer is yes to any of these things, it is okay, but know that you have to move forward.

Yes, you're allowed to be upset. You have the right to feel what you feel, but remind yourself to let it go and keep moving forward. Continue to follow what you have to do in your schedule, and don't allow yourself to shut down in misery or anger. "The show must go on." Your day must go on. It is okay to have weak moments, but mentally and emotionally pushing through to complete what you had already committed to is a practice in persistence. No person, argument, or even bad luck is worth losing your positive energy over. Your life will not complete what you had scheduled to get done without you.

The type of energies I'm attracted to are vibrant conversations. Conversations that I gain value from. Conversations that I'm learning different thought perspectives from. Conversations that make me want to ask questions. Moreless, accomplishments, growth, growing pains, and humor are all engaging to me, and I love to get lost in it. Humor and comedy can go a long way in connecting with others (especially with everything happening in the current political and social climate). Comedy fills a void that allows laughter to release all that negative energy and tension that occurs mentally and physically.

Per Stephen Colbert, "You can't laugh and be afraid at the same time."

Comedy is a way to bust through fear. It is a way to process fear and the unknown. So take a dive into comedy. It can remind you not to take life so seriously, and to always be present.

When I was working for the TV show, "The Last O.G.", every morning I would take Tracy Morgan to set. He would have his speaker in one hand blasting old school music, as he greeted every crew member he passed on his way. He created such a positive atmosphere that every crew member looked forward to coming to work. This was important because not only do we spend long days together, but it can take a physical toll on us which joy can make far more tolerable. Olyvia Diaz, a Chicago hairstylist, told me it is important to wake up 4 out of the 7 days of the week happy, looking forward to work. If you already do this, this is your reminder that you are on track!

On the other hand, negative energy can create a very different experience. Not waking up excited for work and being surrounded by co-workers who do not love what they do is a sign that you may be heading in the wrong direction. When I see co-workers deal with customers and they continue to argue versus creating a solution for the customer to leave happy, I get frustrated and annoyed. It troubles me that people bring the situation down rather than looking to create a solution. When I experience negative energy, I learn about myself: what I will and will not tolerate. This is for the sake of protecting my own energy.

When people have a good aura and energy, not only do I automatically connect with them, but I also feel comfortable allowing them to advise and guide me. It is only those who I feel have good, positive energy that I really allow to provide any guiding advice related to my career.

I have implemented the principles of living a F.E.A.R.L. E.S.S. journey. I have had the pleasure to meet T. Sean Ferguson and his A.D. family team (Marcos Gonzalez Palma, Eric Giarratano, Alex Summers, and Derek Peterson) after having only lived in New York a short while. Not only has he welcomed me onto his team (which means whatever job he works on he is able to bring me along with him), but he has taught me valuable career-based lessons. I will forever love and truly appreciate him. The fact that he takes the time out of his day to teach me things, like how to break down a script and how to create storyboards on movie magic.

How Sean teaches me to be fearless is by learning as much as I can from everyone I have worked with, and learn from mistakes that I have made on every job. I aim to learn as much as I can on and off set. In doing so, I will be able to apply everything I have absorbed. When Sean walks onto the set, he gains so much respect, and the crew listens to him because he is very knowledgeable, and an expert at his job.

Another way I learned how energy is an important tool in your fearless journey is from the interviews I've conducted. When I interviewed Amaury Nolasco, he described how his connection with God acted as his energy engine. Energy is a spiritual guide for him that he incorporates in his everyday routine. From the time he wakes up, he thanks the Lord for an amazing day he is about to have. He prays and thanks God prior to every meal before he eats, and thanks the Lord before he shoots every scene on set. Knowing he gets his energy from

God, he thrives and is grateful for every moment, especially when he is blessed to stay busy as an actor.

However, not everyone seeks spiritual guidance or feels energized in spiritually based energy. Another perspective I appreciate is that of Olyvia Diaz. She explains how energy influences one's hectic lifestyle, and that we have to balance our energy. Your energy is a reflection of how you are doing.

This is similar to Allen Maldonado's perspective in that you know when you have positive and/or negative energy happening within because you have the self awareness. Anytime you realize you have negative energy within yourself, do not allow yourself to dampen that energy in a room. The last thing you want to do is spread your melancholy aura and damage other people's good aura and energy.

Olyvia further elaborates that sometimes people may not understand their own needs and energy in a given moment. She claims clients often come sit in her chair and are not looking for answers or reasons. They simply want something that doesn't exist. She gives them just that by reading their energy and understanding what they're feeling. Sometimes she will give her clients exactly what they do not want and they will still be happy because that is what they came in for: for her to fill a void that brings them both awareness and happiness. She explains that sometimes people do not know what they want until they sit there, but if she is open to them, she is able to still fill their needs successfully.

All in all, be aware how you manage your energy.

CHAPTER 4

AWARENESS

"Life is what happens to you while you're
busy making other plans."

(John Lennon)

Awareness is knowing and not knowing at the same time. I always knew I wanted to be in the entertainment industry, but I did not know exactly what position I wanted to have. Regardless, having the awareness to always push myself forward and be determined and hungry to learn more led me closer to what I love. That same awareness can bring that clarity to you.

To start, gaining your awareness of what you love, think about your own life. Which industry catches your attention? What topics intrigue you enough to want to learn more about them? What are you good at that you can explore further? Continue to start asking questions like these to yourself, no matter who you are, what resources you have, and where you come from. Do not let anything, nor any-one, hold you back.

Having career options and seeing a ladder of opportunity were always what caught my attention. This is why I ultimately chose the entertainment industry, because there's always room to keep growing. Of course, this didn't happen overnight. It took me living in three different cities, and many more job opportunities, to really find out what I wanted to do, to have, and to realize it is still evolving. Awareness during your own journey will allow you to be F.E.A.R.L.E.S.S. You will know where you want to go and what direction to keep moving for-ward. You will allow yourself to be thrown into the deep and swimming with your discomforts. You will allow yourself for change and learn your limits to get there.

In my own journey, I went from wanting to be a math teacher capturing the attention of a classroom to now wanting to be a 1st Assistant Director and Producer. I want to create and manage the logistics of sets. I want to take care of crew and cast. I also want to assist Directors for millions of viewers to enjoy the art of cinematography. I never would have got-ten here without my awareness of losing interest in a teaching program. I didn't allow myself to keep moving down a path I didn't really want.

My advice to you is to learn for yourself what you are interested in doing in your career. Do not let others tell you what they think you would or would not like. Instead, I advise for you to create life experiences for yourself so you can form your own opinions. I've met a lot of people who told me, "You're going to love the weather in L.A." "The people in New York are mean and the people in L.A. are fake." I appreciate their perspectives based on their experiences, or what they have personally heard. But, if I would have listened to everyone's opinions, I may not have lived in those three different cities that gave me the opportunities.

It's not just an awareness of your interests that's important. Another type of awareness to incorporate into your fearless journey is the importance of gratitude. In my interview with Amaury Nolasco, another actor I was blessed to have worked with, he mentions how his wonderful family reminds him where he comes from, and seeing how they live is a reminder that everything he has can all be gone in a heartbeat. The people he loves, the work, the opportunities-they are not guaranteed even once you've "made it."

Amaury has experienced being on top, consistently busy with work, and being healthy as an actor. On the other hand, he has also experienced much sadness, the frustration of not consistently working, and even being quite sick. I have personally witnessed him being sick and feeling vulnerable. Knowing I saw him in those conditions reminded him that humans are not invincible and we are at God's mercy.

What Amaury felt reminded me when one day I woke up for work and out of no where I couldn't move my neck. I had no idea why this was happening to me and immediately got scared because I need to work in order to pay the bills. I have never been so sore and vulnerable before when I felt this type of pain. Feeling this neck pain reminded me to be blessed to have a neck and have the ability to move my neck. I also realized that I overworked my body and my body was calling for help.

We will not be here forever. Remind yourself that we are all on our own fearless journeys, and it does not help us to put pressure on ourselves or others when things get difficult or challenging. Remind yourself to not harm others when you're mad, to help others when they're in need, and do what you are meant to do in this world. Remember to be aware of your mortality and compassionate of those around you.

Allow your awareness to come from deep within you and what you've learned in your life. Allow your awareness to open up your vision. Allow yourself to map out the steps to get you where you want to go. Prepare yourself for change that *will* happen and be open to that change. Allow yourself to grow and to make mistakes. Allow yourself to trust where you are and where your awareness comes from.

Tell yourself that yes, you can. Yes, you can adapt whether change happens with money, health, or work. When you allow this to happen, you will then understand how awareness becomes a part of your fearless journey, to get you where you want to be. You will realize that being fearless isn't about not just having any fear, but having fear and going forward anyway.

An exercise I recommend, no matter what stage you are in finding what you love to do, tell yourself every day that now is your time. Create a daily ritual to remind yourself that it is time you allow yourself to adapt to change. It is okay to be scared. For example, I was afraid to write this book because of the challenges, finances, time commitment, and investment required to make it happen. It didn't matter. Making yourself happy versus making other people was my new rule. I pushed myself past my perceived limit because I did not want life to pass me by without doing what I really wanted to do.

Speaking of life passing you by, try something else. Do you drive? If your answer is yes, is there a route from Point A to Point B that you know blindly because you have driven that route thousands of times before? Can you get to your destination with your eyes closed? Now, have you ever driven this same route that you know backwards and forwards from the passenger seat during this same exact trip? If you haven't yet, try it.

Once you have done it, what new perspective did you have as a passenger? Did you notice new restaurants? Did you actually look at your surroundings and observe the world? What about realizing something that was there all along but just seeing now? While being the driver, you think you are observing it all, but really your mind is concerned with the road, traffic lights, pedestrians, or the gas gauge, and not solely on your surroundings.

The point of this exercise is to quit always being the driver when it comes to your life. Stop and learn how to take a break from your driver's seat when it concerns work, bills, school, or social drama. Learn how to balance life from the passenger's seat, a new perspective from time to time. Enjoy and observe where life is taking you. Be present. Be aware, and live your life as you enjoy the ride. Practicing this will ensure you do not allow your life to just pass you by.

Another perspective of awareness that I've learned is to "be obsessed with success" and what you do. People who love what they do are truly obsessed with what they do. Take Kobe Bryant. When Kobe has to shoot a commercial, you can almost guarantee that there will be a basketball hoop on set so he can shoot free throws in between takes. The practice helps to center and ground him. He also wakes up every morning at 4:00 AM to do conditioning workouts to keep his body strong. He may not want to wake up at 4:00 AM every day, but he does it to ensure his place on his NBA team is safe, and he is strong enough to continue being a great player. People who are great at what they do are obsessed with what they do.

Of course, it is important as an athlete to train physically for your job. However, what is also necessary, whether you are an athlete or not, is to train your mind. Allen Maldonado once told me, "You are what your most dominant thoughts are." He applied this to his life by surrounding himself with images and representations of things that he wanted to achieve. So when he woke up, he would flood his mind with all of his goals. He surrounded himself with what he wanted his thoughts to be: positive reinforcements of where he was headed.

After conducting many interviews with varying actors and even reflecting on my own fearless journey, an important question that I asked myself is this: "How do you fall back in love with what you love to do?" This question was important because my answer could lead me to leaving my current career path. Or, I could learn how to fall back in love with my current role and journey.

For me, I realize that I enjoy living on the edge and exploring new places. However, once I caught myself in a comfortable routine, even though I was shooting in different physical locations, meeting different people, and learning new things, I was starting to lose interest.

By losing interest for even a short period of time, I started questioning my every move. So, after applying what I've learned, I was committed to falling back in love with what I do. I started to ask more questions on set. I printed out pictures and posted them in my room. I made a visual timeline and goal calendar for myself, so I could start living more in the moment versus thinking so far ahead.

By doing all of this, I realized some people are able to process once they realize they no longer enjoy doing what they do, and they can immediately change occupations. In my case, I just knew I had cold feet about becoming complacent and decided to fall in love with my work again.

Falling in love what you do again and again is not convincing yourself or continuing to do the wrong thing. What I learned is I was slightly taking what I do for granted while being very self aware of my feelings and commitment to my job. Most importantly, I got to remember why I love what I do and let those memories come back to rekindle my fire.

What are your wants? How do you keep yourself aware? Without keeping track of these two questions, Olyvia Diaz feels she would not be able to sustain her own level of success. One way of sustaining herself is her morning routines. If she does not start her day feeling grounded with the practices of self-care and setting her daily intentions, she cannot help others. She understands that without feeling grounded in the morning, she will be playing catch up with her own feelings for the remaining of the day.

Take care of yourself and stay true to your needs. Allow your awareness to include what sort of needs you have. These needs can translate into whatever routine you need to sustain yourself before helping others.

Being aware of how you adapt to change is very important, because how well you adapt to change will reflect on how far you will go out of your comfort zone, and how many risks you will allow yourself to take. Set yourself up to win, and always be continuously aware.

CHAPTER 5

RISK

"The big risk bring the big rewards..."

(Karen Stuckey)

Risks-I am not suggesting you risk your life, or to put yourself in danger. Risk-when you are putting your self out there and you truly do not know what your outcome will be. A calculated risk equals rewards.

In Chapter 1, you learned my story. I went from wanting to be a school teacher to becoming a Communication Media & Theater major and then, immediately after college, I took a risk to follow my dreams. I left my whole life in Chicago to move to a city I'd only visited once before. I moved to L.A. and then eventually finding my way to New York. I genuinely did not know what the outcome of any of those choices would be. The only goal was to find my passion and be successful at it. I set no other option for myself.

Similar to my path, Amaury Nolasco also changed careers. You typically hear the story that all actors knew they wanted to be one since they were very young. For Amaury, his career turning point happened during his process of becoming a doctor. With his father, mother, and brother all being doctors, that was what his mind was set on. He was going to become a doctor and follow the family legacy.

Instead, Amaury's calling for acting found him. When the opportunity came to him out of the blue, which was during the same time he was becoming a biology major, he had that internal "a-ha" moment. His gut feeling told him this was something he should try, and to set aside the family legacy for the time being. He listened to his gut instinct and it turned out to be the right path for him.

Recognizing this internal feeling is one thing. But for Amaury, telling his family his plans for a major career change was scary. To his surprise, he got their love and support to do it. The only thing he didn't get from them was the financial support. It didn't matter. In his gut, he still knew he was making the right decision.

During these moments of realization, not only are you listening to your instincts, but you may be experiencing a feeling that this decision you are about to make feels right, based on no evidence at all. Have you ever felt this before?

From my own experience with taking risks, my financial state was something I could not consider if I was looking to take a risk. I would not have moved to Los Angeles or New York if I had let money be the determining factor. Why? I went to L.A. with only $500 in my bank account. I still owed money on my credit cards and when I moved to New York, I had only about $1,000 to my name.

Regardless of your current financial standing, do not let your bank accounts scare you into changing your mind. Change your thinking to motivate yourself. Have positive thoughts that you can do this and you can afford it. Allow only positive thoughts regarding the reward that taking this big risk can create for you. If you feel that your fear is breaking you down, pivot that negative perspective into the positive.

For Amaury, when he began to feel unsure, negative, or doubtful about whether he was making the right decision, his father advised him to go to Old San Juan and talk to the elders. He believed that they could give him some valuable insight into living life to its fullest potential.

After Amaury explored and asked questions, his key take-away was, "No regrets, just jump." He weaved this mantra into his own perspective to relate to his own life. He knew he could become a doctor, but not an actor. He could not live wondering, so he took the advice to heart. It's not about taking a risk for the sake of doing something.

It's important to keep this story in mind when you start to tell yourself you *need* to take a risk. Don't tell yourself that. I have learned that forcing risk for the hope of an opportunity means you are already afraid. Even using the word 'risk' may add anxiety. It's not about taking a risk for the sake of doing something. It's about following your instincts and passions that can appear without warning and for no clear reason. Therefore, rather than using the word 'risk,' tell yourself, "No regrets, just jump, and leave with your pockets full of dreams!" A favorite phrase of mine from Amaury Nolasco.

Aside from experiencing gut feelings, you typically experience this internal moment when you are hungry for more in your life and you are really putting yourself out there. When you are pushing yourself to your limits, you are out of your comfort zone. You are challenging yourself. Without discomfort, you are not allowing yourself to experience risks that can possibly change your life. When you want something, it will happen for you, but you must also be willing to go for it, work very hard and continue to put the work in.

You would think that taking a risk would create more fear of the outcome, or possibly create a narrative that there would not be the light at the end of the tunnel. But ironically, a reward magically comes to you and makes clear to you the reason your gut was screaming so loudly. Understanding this can also lead you to understand yourself. Specifically, understanding what your hobbies are versus your career.

It is important to remember that everyone has hobbies. Hobbies are different than your career. Yes, hobbies can lead to developing your career or help you determine a decision, but distinguishing what you like versus what you love to do every day is important. If you didn't get paid to do it, will you still continue to do it? Taking a risk can lead to uncovering the truth about something that you want to be your hobby versus your career.

Imagine you win the lottery and you win enough to be financially set for life and don't need to work for the rest of your life. I can honestly and personally say I would still continue to work in production because I love what I do. Many of the actors I work with have said the same: they love what they do so much that they will continue to act even if they didn't need the paycheck.

Similar to the risk of having to leave family, in Allen Maldonado's case, the hood was all he knew. His brothers were not bad individuals, they were merely living their lives accustomed to how they were raised. For Allen, he risked leaving his family, community, and his sense of security because he did not want to live the lifestyle he was born into. He had to separate himself from his neighborhood brothers in order to achieve something different.

To change you have to remove yourself from situations that don't serve your end goals. One way to do this quickly is simply to take yourself out of your comfort zone. In order to do this, you must know where and what your comfort zones are. Really dig deep and find these answers within yourself. By doing so, you will start your growing pain process.

Without applying the risk of pushing outside of our comfort zone, we won't be able to achieve a higher level of success and satisfaction in our careers. We have to be fearless and jump.

Introducing myself to crew and knocking on production truck doors when I saw them in New York City was definitely risky. When I lived in Chicago and Los Angeles, I never saw production trucks, but in New York I saw them a lot. After getting the response from crew that I stood out by doing this, they gained respect for me even though they didn't know me or work with me before. It was my (successful) attempt to show them a glimpse of my character and work ethic.

Risk created respect for me, which then followed with open doors of opportunity. As new opportunities unfolded one after another in the entertainment industry created an oppurtunity for me to meet. It created a chance for me to meet additional key players on set who were genuinely pleased to work with me. Risk, in my life, led to respect as long as my intentions were pure.

Here is an exercise I want you to try. It can be in your current city or you can make a trip out of it and travel to a new city or country you see yourself wanting to live. I recommend you go by yourself. If you chose to stay where you live, go to buildings, houses, apartments, lofts, or condos in an area where, if you had the funds, you would purchase. When you get to the area, get lost in the architecture, culture, environment, but most importantly, get lost in a calm state of mind - become a tourist.

As you are soaking everything in with your bare eyes, tell yourself, "I will make it. If people who currently live here can do it, I can do it, too. Because I know this, no one can stop me." I've done this exercise while living in New York and Los Angeles. I manifested to practice my potential and learn as much as I can in each city.

I did not want to live a lifestyle by what social media is portraying what or how it should be. Instead, I put the effort to learn how to receive income by doing what I love to do. This lifestyle I grew into I am proud of and I am genuinely happy to wake up every morning to go to work. The result of my manifestation is uncanny. Your beautiful fearless mind is your tool to make life happen for yourself.

If you decided to take a trip for this exercise, you will learn that even booking your trip alone was a risk. You take a risk by visiting a place that came from an idea in your mind. You put action behind your idea. But, not only did you apply action, you formed your own opinion about the place you traveled to based on your personal experience. This is huge and you should be proud of yourself.

This exercise can create two totally different experiences. However, with these exercises you applied risk in an effort to grow your comfort zone just a little bigger.

Like Olyvia states, "Life is too short. You have to risk it for the biscuit." In other words, go out and get it. You don't know what else is out there because you haven't been willing to do what it takes to know. Lose the word "but" in your vocabulary and see what results unfold when your excuses are gone.

What I didn't realize until after interviewing people is that they all had taken significant risks from something that happened to them personally. One lost a sister. Another almost died in a car accident. Another was a Type 1 diabetic since they were two years old. Even though they had different personal situations at different times in their lives, these personal matters lead them to take their risk leaps.

What risks do you get to take? Is it your health? Is it love? Is it your vulnerability? Is it your morals? Is it what you believe in?

Risks can be taken in so many areas of our lives. We may not know what risk we need to take to push our lives forward. What are you willing to give? What are you willing to do, to prove, or reach the life of your dreams?

People are often worried about the process versus the results. Sometimes, the risk is not taking one. The risk is a way of getting to a new place and putting yourself on the journey or not. You can sit in your bunker forever. However, it is up to you, whether or not you are going to see what a storm brings in and stare at the rubble. Or, if you decide to fight through the storm and make new.

Risk is about fearlessness and finding out for yourself what you love. It's allowing yourself to strengthen your risk-taking muscles, and dig deep with your research and outreach to figure out how to do what you love. It is simply allowing yourself to be vulnerable. When you are vulnerable in this case, you are giving yourself wiggle room to grow and being patient with time.

We live in a world where we often hear time is money, I don't have enough time to do x, y, and z, or there simply isn't enough time in the day. Therefore, the moral of this is remind you to give yourself time, because it does take time. In this journey you are doing your research. You are putting your whole heart in it and getting a taste of how it feels. Whatever you feel, whatever you love, do more of that. In my case, I was on a constantly risky journey. Your own happiness is worth it. Take those risks. Do not let anyone convince you to think differently.

Chapter 6

Lessons

"What is your next big move?"

(Tabitha De La O)

When I get asked what my next move is, I often feel I need to know the answer, even if other people aren't asking yet. However, when my sister asks me this question I look at it differently. After all, I believe my family members are my first teachers.

I am sure we all have learned lessons both in and outside of a classroom. A big lesson for me was making time for myself (your "you time"). I was putting other people's happiness and needs over my own. When you lose sight of your routines and stop doing things that make you happy on a daily basis, you quickly start to feel it mentally, emotionally, and physically. With this said, I've learned that I will always be there for people that I love. The key lesson though is making sure I get done whatever I need to do before giving anyone my word or presence.

Another lesson is to take a moment to look back, and reflect on how much you accomplished. Once you sync that in, your next step is, where are you currently? This step is giving yourself the reminder you need to know if are you on track or not. In other words, are you where you want to be right now? The lesson I learned in not doing this is that you are not tracking your career progress. By not tracking your career progress, you lose your motivation and drive to find your passion.

How far are you on your to-do list? Are you completing your tasks? It is important not only to complete a task, but to complete the task correctly. There is a difference. Doing it right means reprioritizing, rethinking, and stopping to restart it, if need be. But no matter what, remind yourself to never get too stubborn or too prideful to admit when you need to start over.

Just as time keeps going, lessons never stop either. Accepting that I will continue to make mistakes helped me to no longer feel anxious when I started new opportunities. I made mistakes every day, yet learned new things as well. However, I never made the same mistake twice.

Training yourself not to make the same mistake twice allows you to mentally keep growing and get past it. You learn from your mistake instead of dwelling on it. By doing so, you will start gaining trust in yourself, which will then even help you feel more confident when making your own decisions.

Decision Making

What is your decision-making process like? What I mean by this is, do you make your own decisions, or do you still lean on your parents, spouse, etc. to help make your decisions? When you get asked something, does it go through your own critical thinking filter first, or do you call mom, dad, sister, brother, or your mentor for their input?

If you realize that going to someone else is your default, this may not be an easy change for you. Moving forward, I challenge you to filter through your own critcal thinking filter first when it comes to your next decision. Allow yourself a minute to form your own opinion and decision. By doing so, you are becoming your own fearless decision maker.

Does age matter?

I was recently asked, "Do you think fearlessness has to do with age?" - which opened up a learning opportunity for me. Before writing this book, my target audience was Millennials. I originally thought that they are hungrier than ever to become successful and are really committed to it. However, after interviewing different people with different titles in the industry, I have learned that age is irrelevant in fearlessness. A fearless journey can start at any age.

Even though success can start at different stages of life, we live in a world where people constantly compare themselves to one another. It is easy to do when we often have mobile devices nearby to access media content. People are constantly scrolling on Instagram, Facebook, Twitter, and Snapchat, not even realizing that they are comparing their lives and level of success or happiness, to others. I am guilty of doing this myself. But you come to realize, after a certain amount of time, that social media isn't healthy for you. You will catch yourself resenting your growing pains and continue to compare your journey with other people's success. There are studies that prove how unhealthy this can be for us, and yet the addiction can be hard to walk away from.

I am not saying go and delete all of your social media accounts. Instead, be aware how many hours a day you are on social media. If you are starting your day by grabbing your phone and immediately checking your social media pages, you'll be using your valuable time to compare instead of developing relationships or putting in the hard work we've already discussed in this book. Don't distract yourself like that. Instead, allow someone positive to distract your mind through a book or a podcast. Or, curate your pages with positive messages from thoughtful leaders and successful individuals you strive to be like, to keep you motivated and hungry for success.

No matter how old you are, don't be afraid to ask questions. I don't know why people get afraid to ask questions, especially when we're younger. We don't have the experience to know it all, yet! Asking questions has only made me into a stronger employee. When you are dealing with budgets, logistics, time, people, and other important tasks that others rely on you to handle, you have every right to ask questions. Of course, similar to not making the same mistake again, I also try not to ask the same question twice, unless there is a unique situation occurring.

Aside from not being afraid to ask questions, another important lesson is learning the triggers for your feelings and knowing how to control them. You and only you have the power over them. Your feelings are part of your personal seeds, and you have every right to feel them.

Therefore, when it comes to your personal seeds, always protect and embrace them. Your personal seeds are placed in your garden. To protect your seeds, do not just let anyone enter your garden gate and water your plants with ill intentions. In other words, your body is your garden so protect it and guard it on your fearless journey.

I am still on my journey to evolve more and more everyday. This journey has been both a blessing and hard work. When I catch myself struggling or beating myself up, or at times complaining about the little things, I remember the advice to not take opportunities for granted.

Treasure every moment of your career and life. Even if you catch yourself not enjoying an experience, rather than complain about it and feel miserable, learn to embrace it, take it in, and move on to let the experience fully unfold.

Make every experience of your life a lesson. Learning from your mistakes and triumphs leads to fearlessness. So when you make a mistake, you learn and move forward. When you achieve something big, you overcome obstacles. By doing so, you are more apt to take risks because you know that there is always something to learn from the experience, no matter how it turns out.

Chapter 7

Effort

Me: "What is your Plan B?"

Amaury Nolasco : "To make Plan A work."

Put in the effort with who you are working with. In my case, that looks like head of departments, assistant directors, producers, unit production managers, directors, actors, mentors, cast, and crew. The result I have gotten after putting effort in has driven me to find out what I love to do. I am blessed and busy.

Being a freelancer and not knowing what, or where, your next job is living on the edge, yet trusting the process of it. At the same time, it gives you the power to put all your effort into meeting new people and leaving your imprint on them.

My current goal is to make sure everybody on and off set knows my name on every job I get. The entertainment industry is so big, yet you always see similar faces in production when you go from job to job. Putting in the time to go the extra mile and have a personal conversation with each person could mean that my resume gets prioritized over someone else's someday.

Aside from putting the effort into making sure everybody knows my name, my time also plays a factor. Realizing that your time is a valuable asset because you can never get back time, you start prioritizing personal goals and creating deadlines for yourself. You then start to become more efficient with your time. Without making deadlines, I am less likely to complete the tasks or complete the short and long term goals I set for myself.

Creating deadlines, managing your time, and continuing to make an effort everyday has to be consistent. Consistency is key. Your consistencies lead to your habits. It takes 22 days for something to become a habit.

Because I have a different schedule every day, it is impossible to have an identical or ideal routine. With this said, the following things are what I make sure I squeeze into my daily routine:

- I start my day by drinking a glass of water and thanking God for another day.
- If my call time is before 7:00 AM, I make sure to hit the gym after a 12+hour workday, even if it's only for a 20-minute run.

- I glimpse at my to-do list for the day so I have an idea of what personal tasks I have to get done, aside from my workload. While I am at work, I am mentally at work and not distracted by what is going on in my personal life.
- During my lunch, I make sure I call my sisters, mom, and dad. Whether they answer or not, I reach out to them daily.
- Once my 12-18 hour workday is over, I come home, hit the sauna if I didn't do it that morning, and wash my face. I end my day by drinking a glass of water and then drinking a cup of green tea right before I go to sleep.
- Repeat!

This routine may seem boring, but after building an understanding of how production hours affect my body and my mind, I have created a routine that best supports my needs to keep me in top shape. Most importantly, I am sure not to neglect my physical health. I am a true believer that without your health, you have nothing. It is important to have energy and stay fit.

But health is not the only way to ground yourself and keep focused. I remember asking Amaury what his strategy was in making an effort to get more work again when things got slow. Did he have to rewind and go back to square one, like when he first started his acting career? His response was that in the beginning, it felt effortless. His process over time was approaching each opportunity and seeing what did or didn't work based off what he already knew. When you apply what you already know, you start getting a handle on your career hub. During this process, you'll realize you can pivot your career perspective. By doing so, you are putting effort to reconnect with everyone you know who can help you. Regardless of what happens, you keep moving forward after falling off your horse. No matter what happens and how many times you fall, you must tell yourself that you are the only one with the power to get back on the saddle.

Amaury mentioned how he always had the mentality of having only a "Plan A." If he was ever asked, "What his Plan B was?" his consistent answer was "to make sure Plan A works."

After hearing this, I recognized this mantra in my own life. When I first moved to L.A. right after college, I was starting from scratch and learning the system and industry. After leaving Los Angeles, I got comfortable and stopped putting in effort, resulting in me falling off my horse. Then being in Chicago, I applied what I already knew and forced myself right back in that saddle. By doing so, it led me to visit New York. Since I had no network at first in the entertainment industry in New York, oppurtunity didn't happen for me right away. Therefore, I had to go back to square one in my relationship-building process. But, thankfully, I wasn't back at square one in my industry, because I already had the confidence and some experience under my belt.

When applying what I learned in two different cities, I was able to find my stride and I've been riding my horse out in New York for almost two years now. Applying the advice to not take my career and/or any experiences for granted nor accepting defeat, I have been busy and blessed.

Being a creature of habit and having a systematic routine is important. If your environment is messy, your life is messy. Your thought process happens mentally, but more specifically it reflects your thought process. Being as organized as possible and making sure you are getting things done is key to maintaining the habit of positive thinking. When you apply effort to this you are creating your line of work, sales, relationships, and other future opportunities.

Exercises:

Cold Calling:

I mentioned in Chapter 1 how my efforts with cold calling definitely made an impact on the way I found work and opportunities. Cold calls opened several doors no matter what city I was in.

Cold calling is a practice that feels fairly risky to people. A lot of people fear cold calling, because they fear the rejection on the other side. This is an important part of your effort to creating your line of work, sales, relationships, and other opportunities. So, here are some steps to cold calling successfully.

Step 1: First, pick what industry you want to reach out to in your own city: accounting, marketing, public relations, law, production, pharmaceuticals, corporate, etc. Once you choose one...

Step 2: Google the top 10 companies in that industry in the city you live and/or choose to work in.

Step 3: Create a spreadsheet with several columns. You'll want to list the name of the company, the phone number, an email address, and any related notes.

Step 4: Make sure you have your resume finalized and ready to send. Keep in mind that you may need to tweak it a little bit to customize for each person or company you send it to.

Step 5. After looking through the website of some of these companies, start putting the information in your excel document. You'd be surprised how quickly this list adds up.

Step 6: Once you have information on 10-20 companies information inputted in your excel file, start calling them one by one. Follow the dialogue below in the beginning, and I am sure after five calls you will be able to make them without the script. Here is what worked for me:

> *"Hi my name is Sammy. If I was interested in working with your company, who would be the best contact to reach to send my resume and/or possibly have an info session with?"*

Approximately 99% of the time, the receptionist will give you that contact person's name and email address. They will also know if the company is currently looking to hire people. Hiring or not, make sure you get connected and give your email address directly to the person the receptionist mentioned. It is equally important to make sure you get that receptionist's name! Once you get it, type it in the notes section in your excel file (you will see later why this is important). Before the receptionist transfers you over, make sure they give you an email address first to send your resume to, just in case the person they transfer you to doesn't pick up. Not only are you able to leave a voicemail, but then you can also email your resume immediately afterwards.

If you have to leave a voicemail, you can say the following:

> *"Hi, my name is [insert name here]. I was referred by [receptionist's name] to contact you and to send my resume. I am reaching out to you at this time regarding a possible position to work for your company. If you are hiring now, I would love the opportunity to have an info session with you."*

Step 7: Once you have ended the call, you will now email your resume. The subject of your email will be: the person's name the receptionist told you to contact - referred by [receptionist's name] - [your name]'s resume.

Example:

Haley Producer - referred by Jane Secretary –
Sammy De La O's Resume

The body of your email should look something like this.

Hi (Person's name),

If they spoke to you on the phone:
It was a pleasure to talk to you via phone today, (put date).

I appreciate you taking the time to speak to me and providing information about your company to me.

OR

If they didn't answer and you left a voicemail, or if the receptionist only gave you an email to contact and did not transfer you to voicemail:

Today, (put date), I was told by (receptionist name) to reach out to you in regards to a possible work position in your company if you had any available.

Like I promised (receptionist name), attached in this email is my resume.

If they told you they are not currently hiring:

I know you mentioned your company is not currently hiring. However, I wanted to still send you my resume just in case anything ever opened up in the future, you would have my information on file.

OR

If they told you they are looking to hire:

I look forward to hearing back from you. If you need anything else from me, please let me know.

Again, thank you for your time and have a great rest of your week.

Best,
(Your name)

This exercise has worked for me in each city that I've worked. So, I am confident that it will work for you as well.

I have learned over time that not a lot of people have this skill set anymore, the art of cold calling. But I hope after reading this section, you will no longer be afraid to give it a shot for yourself.

Routines to apply to yourself: you need to expand efforts not only on people and your career, but you, yourself.

1. Journaling
   - Start traveling everywhere you go with a pen and a mini notebook, or use your notes app on your phone. Start writing and logging what is crossing your mind everyday.
2. Meditation
   - Download free meditation apps, follow along, and do at least 5 minutes of meditation. Or if the app doesn't work for you, just lay down and turn off all electronics around you, and start breathing in and out slowly.
3. Working out
   - Hit the gym, office workouts, at home workouts, etc.
4. Listening to music
   - Create your playlist and start getting lost in your music.
5. Having a sacred space
   - It can be a beach, your room, your car, library, coffee shop, yoga class, etc. This is your area, where you release all negative thoughts and energy. Once

you have released all the negativity in your body, the positivity starts pumping in and all around your body. In this space of yours, you are simply the best version of yourself, because nothing can bring you down.

Putting the time into these routines will create a balance for you. We are human. We can't just work, work, and work all the time. By putting effort into yourself (mind and body), you will be rewarded with the gift of harmony and peace. Creating that harmony and peace within yourself will increase your effort levels on all of your career and personal platforms. Your energy and your effort are crucial to being fearless.

CHAPTER 8

STORY

"Create your story and allow life to unfold."

(Silva Hernandez)

At the beginning of this book, I told you about my story and myself. The reasoning of this was to gain your trust before you read these lessons about fearlessness, and to begin your F.E.A.R.L.E.S.S. journey. By sharing my story with you, it gives you context of why my message to you is valuable, and gives me the opportunity to be vulnerable with you.

With this said, are you sharing your story? Or do you only tell your story if you are asked about it?

If you are, great! Whom are you sharing it with? What has resulted from sharing your story? If you're not sharing your story, why not? Do you feel that your story isn't unique? Do you feel guilty about talking about yourself? Do you feel that your story does not have value due to not taking risks in your life? Are you afraid to be vulnerable?

There is no incorrect answers to these questions. The questions are for you to realize what is getting in the way of telling your story, so you are living your life to its potential and inspiring others to do the same. By telling your story, you demonstrate fearlessness because you are expressing yourself, and showing that you are vulnerable.

People have walls up to protect themselves, and they curtain their fears as if to say, "I am not good enough. It is not good enough. There's not enough." By sharing your story, you are bringing these walls down and creating a common ground to connect with others. You are making your audience feel understood and, at the same time, sharing with the world. If that story is not full of great news and high-level accomplishment (yet), that is okay.

There is only one of you in this world. You are your own uniqueness. Because there is only one of you, there is only one person who can put you out into the world in a way that only you can. You don't need to feel selfish when you are telling your story. I've learned to not feel that way anymore. I'm unclear on why I was feeling that way in the first place. However, I've come to realize that telling your story makes people understand you better, and gives you the opportunity to prove to yourself that it is okay to be vulnerable.

Being vulnerable is proving you are human and life situations do happen. One is when things simply go wrong throughout the entire day. For instance, waking up late for work and then getting into an argument with a close friend. So now you are feeling shitty, you get to work and nothing is going in your favor. By the end of the day you realize you misplaced your keys and now you are locked out of your apartment.

Another example was when I got a midnight call from my dad after getting out of work, and dad told me his sister passed away. Life can pivot in so many directions all at once and leave you feeling many difference types of conflicting emotions. But the lesson behind this is life is part of your story.

Stories are a way people can relate and learn from you.

Even you, yourself, need to hear your story and, from time to time, verbally tell it to yourself. It is great practice for you to start telling it before you tell the world. By practicing in a private space, my story has given me clarity. Clarity on who and what were my biggest prizes in life.

After reading this book, I hope you see that it is time to craft your story, too.

Chapter 9

Success

"Be obsessed with success!"

(Allen Maldonado)

No matter what point in life you are currently at with your career, do you look and see how far you have come?

Celebrating Success:
Do you celebrate your success? How do you celebrate success? I have learned after writing this book, and through my career, that people celebrate it differently. Even just in knowing that success means different things to different people, I gained several perspectives on it.

There is no one blueprint for success. All we can do is simply share our story with those who want to listen, share what we know, and what we do. Each and every one of us has our own blueprint that we develop to determine what makes us successful in our lives.

Success to Amaury looks like his parents being his number one fans, and being alive to witness it. It also looks like celebrating along with his family and friends. But again, success is still writing itself right now and he still has many more things he is aiming to accomplish. Amaury doesn't want to be the shooting star that many other actors and celebrities aspire to be. He wants to be a star that stays up in the sky. Success will stop for him when he quits. Amaury Nolasco is not a quitter.

Before Allen explained what success means to him, he raised an interesting question. "Do fish celebrate when they swim?" No, this is what fish are born and built to do. But this is how he sees himself: he was born and built for what he is currently doing and accomplishing. Therefore, success for him is being efficient, so he can do and provide things for his family. Being able to pay bills, provide clothes and school supplies for his family. Being a provider is success for him. And to Allen, that doesn't require celebration.

For me, celebrating my success is sharing my line of work with my family. I was able to fly my sisters and parents to New York, and welcome them to my line of work. They got the opportunity to meet the amazing cast and crew I worked with. I have learned to turn gifts into experiences.

Another way I celebrate my success is allowing myself to look back at each job I completed. I reflect on how much I have grown, learned, and accomplished from it. Taking time to look back, especially in this business is important, because it helps me not to take my job and life for granted. It becomes the reminder that I need to stay in tune with myself, and on track with my career. I get to celebrate that my career trajectory has been forward, and not backwards or lateral.

Outside of celebrating my career success, another way I celebrate success is with my annual beach summer gathering in Chicago. I bring together, family and friends, to celebrate our bond and friendships. We all share quality time while eating, dancing, cooking, and playing beach volleyball together. It is a time where we don't have to talk about work, while celebrating unity, growth, and encouragement for each other.

Your success comes from within you, just as being fearless does. It is in your hands and in your mind. Like what Allen says, "be obsessed with success," and also realize your successes.

Success is all on you as a human. No one else can define it for you. It doesn't matter how many books you read to become successful, or how much money you have in the bank. It matters how you wake up every morning and what you tell yourself that will make you happy, and feel fulfilled and successful. Just know that this fearless journey will be your first and/or next success story.

CHAPTER 10

YOU ARE WORTH IT

*"Find a job you enjoy, and you will never have
to work a day in your life..."*

(Mark Twain)

I wrote this book for you, the reader. After reading this book, I hope to have offered solutions and exercises for you to now apply to this crazy thing we call life.

Yes, I could have made this book into a web series, blog or some other form of digital content. But we live in a world of constant social media and online based platforms, so I wanted this content to be special. Special enough to disconnect you from all the apps in your life.

I have made it this far on my own by:

- Balancing family and friends
- Managing my energy
- Being self-aware
- Taking risks
- Learning lessons that life taught me
- Putting effort into my life and work
- Expanding those efforts
- Telling my story
- Celebrating my success

Aside from creating and living the life you love, also keep in mind who you want to be. Do what makes you happy every day, and let no one get in the way of it. Keep a steady hobby and routines that will continuously have you grow as a human being. The sky is the limit.

Love people in gallons versus ounces. Fill the void for people mentally, physically, and emotionally. You get to choose who you want to be in this life. Choose fearlessness in all of its glory.

Wherever you are in your life, whether still on the search for your passion or wanting to stretch your plate even more, remind yourself to be F.E.A.R.L.E.S.S. The word "fearless" after today is your new best friend. Fearless is your network, managing your energy, being self-aware, taking risks, learning from your experiences, putting effort into your life and work, sharing your story, and celebrating your success. Use this tool to start or continue to love what you do. You will enhance your vision, but most importantly, you will tap into your fearlessness.

I want you to say the following words out loud:

1. TODAY & EVERYDAY, I AM FEARLESS.
2. STARTING TODAY, I WILL REACH OUT TO MY FRIENDS AND FAMILY MORE OFTEN!
3. I WILL START TO MANAGE MY ENERGY, POS-ITIVE ENERGY!
4. I WILL BE AWARE!
5. I WILL TAKE RISKS!
6. I WILL LEARN FROM MY LESSONS!
7. I WILL EXPEND INTENTIONAL EFFORT!
8. I WILL SHARE MY STORY!
9. I WILL CELEBRATE MY SUCCESS!

Acknowledgments

F.E.A.R.L.E.S.S., my first book, I have been thinking about many people throughout my entire book journey. Many have encouraged me to practice and step into my full potential. Thank you Silvia (Mom), David (Papi), my sisters Tabitha and Mariah, Val and Camille Cavazos, Amaury Nolasco, Allen Maldonado, Olyvia Diaz, Toccara Ross, Juanita Jones Daly, Gina Mo, Noele Contreras, Rocky Quinones, Jay Robles, T. Sean Ferguson, Marcos Gonzalez Palma, Eric Giarratano, Alex Summers, Derek Peterson, Natasha Rivera-Boyle, family, my A.D. Department family, cast and crew family, Bestseller in a Weekend team, LensCrafters family, I also want to thank my book coach, Alicia Dunams, who encouraged me to write and complete my book. The dream of writing my first book wouldn't have come true without you all. Thank you all for supporting me to becoming a first-time author.

I thank my parents for always keeping my sisters and I busy with dance, sports, and family events. Without them and being raised with such a big family, I truly do not believe I would have made it this far in continuing my fearless journey.

About The Author

Sammy "Chicago" De La O is a FEARLESS independent production assistant. She has worked for ABC, Hulu, Amazon, and Netflix Television shows, as well as countless other companies in the entertainment industry.

Sammy recognizes the importance of living fearlessly. Currently, she is a speaker and coach that shares the message of fearlessness, living the life you want, and how to live up to your potential as your life unfolds.

Made in the USA
Middletown, DE
16 July 2019